CLASSIC TRACTION ENGINES

PAUL STRATFORD

HALSGROVE

First published in Great Britain in 2010

British Library Cataloguing-in-Publication Data
A CIP record for this title is available from the British Library

ISBN 978 0 85704 054 1

HALSGROVE
Halsgrove House,
Ryelands Industrial Estate,
Bagley Road, Wellington, Somerset TA21 9PZ
Tel: 01823 653777   Fax: 01823 216796
email: sales@halsgrove.com

Part of the Halsgrove group of companies.
Information on all Halsgrove titles is available at: www.halsgrove.com

Printed and bound by Grafiche Flaminia, Italy

CONTENTS

INTRODUCTION

Over half a century has passed since the legendary 'Race for a Firkin of Ale' took place at Appleford in Oxfordshire in which two pioneers of traction engine preservation, Arthur Napper and Miles Chetwynd-Stapylton raced their fifty-year-old traction engines, head to head for a wager. This was not a public event and to subject two traction engines to the extremes of their mechanical limits would now be judged to be foolhardy, but this event was unwittingly to form the basis for what was to become the traction engine rally as we know today, attracting many thousands of visitors to events throughout the country on most weekends during the summer months.

By the early 1950s production of traction engines had long since ceased and only a few engines, notably steam rollers, were still in revenue earning service. Many engines had long since succumbed to the cutter's torch, but there still remained a considerable number of engines laid aside awaiting their fate in yards, barns and hedgerows around the country. As the preservation movement grew many of these engines would be sold on to enthusiasts, keen not only to preserve our heritage, but also to restore these engines to full working order for future generations to admire and enjoy.

The Road Locomotive Society was formed in 1937 with the aim of encouraging education and research into the history of self propelling road steam engines and vehicles. It was, however, the founding of the National Traction Engine Club (now known as the National Traction Engine Trust) in 1954 that moved forward the idea of the traction engine rally and has since been responsible for a code of practice which promotes, both the safe running of traction engines and traction engine rallies, whilst maintaining the main objective of the trust in *'Preserving our Heritage in Steam on the Road'*.

Over two thousand steam traction engines of all types are known to exist in the UK, not all of which are in running order – some are merely a few rotting remains unlikely if ever to be steamed again – yet each year sees the completion of other long term restoration projects returning what were rusting hulks to their former glory. There is of course a finite number of traction engines remaining worldwide, however even now engines exported to the four corners of the world in the early 1900s are being discovered and repatriated to these shores for restoration.

This volume has been compiled as a pictorial appreciation of the many manufacturers of the steam traction engine, all those early preservationists, current engine owners and enthusiasts who have laboured long and hard to preserve and maintain the steam traction engine for the enjoyment of the past, present and future generations.

Paul Stratford

THE ENGINES

The earliest use of steam power in agriculture was in the form of the portable engine, whereby threshing machines, sawbenches and other machinery would be driven by a belt attached to either the flywheel or the crankshaft pulley of the portable engine. Unlike the later traction engine, the portable engine was not self-propelled and would invariably be moved by horse to different locations. One of only two surviving examples from the Farmers Foundry, 1910-built 7NHP Portable Engine No. 36 simmers away in a quiet corner at Old Warden.

A demonstration of how the diminutive 1868-built Brown & May Portable Engine would have traditionally been moved around using horse power. Note how the chimney has been folded down to improve stability.

The best known of all preserved traction engines, the steam road roller – even today, the modern road roller is still referred to by many as the 'steam roller'. The most prolific of all steam roller manufacturers was Aveling & Porter of Strood in Kent, producing some 8,600 examples of which over four hundred are preserved. The 'prancing horse' emblem and motto 'Invicta' attached to the headstock are taken from the ancient coat of arms of Kent. Suitably workstained Aveling & Porter 10 ton roller No. 9128 built in 1920 looks at home in this contractor's yard in Worcestershire.

The agricultural or general purpose engine could carry out a variety of tasks, powering belt-driven agricultural machinery, hauling loaded trailers and for those fitted with a winch, extracting timber from inaccessible woodland. The sole surviving example from manufacturer Robinson & Auden 6NHP single cylinder engine no.1376 built in 1900 is a fine example of this type of engine. The metal straked rear wheels gave good grip on the untarred roads of the day, but are largely unsuitable for today's hardfaced tarmac road surfaces, offering less adhesion and a rough ride for the crew members.

Above: The introduction of the steam wagon gave operators greater flexibility and shorter journey times whilst affording crews with a greater level of comfort. Foden along with Sentinel were the largest producer of steam wagons, both however finally giving up production of steam-powered wagons in favour of the more user-friendly internal combustion engine powered variant. Early Fodens had the cylinders and motionwork mounted above the boiler and were known as 'overtypes', whilst later models had the 'engine' mounted beneath the chassis and were known as 'undertypes'. Seen here is 'undertype' 6 Ton Foden Wagon Works No. 13178 built in 1929.

Opposite: The road locomotive is a much larger and more powerful type of engine used primarily for hauling large and heavy loads either on a large single trailer or smaller multiple trailers of the type seen here hauled by Fowler A6 Road Locomotive No.13141 built in Leeds in 1913. The Fowler is a two cylinder compound engine, which was not only powerful, but also economical and with the additional belly water tanks could cover greater distances without the need for frequent water stops. The half canopy offered the crew some protection from wet weather whilst still affording good visibility.

Steam tractors were a smaller, lighter and more nimble version of the road locomotive and after a changes in the law in 1903 and 1904 engines under 5 tons were permitted to be driven by one driver; subsequently this was raised to 7¼ tons in 1923. An ideal engine for the road haulage contractor, easy and economic to operate. This 4NHP single cylinder tractor 'So Be It', Works No. 4083 was one of the last examples built by Charles Burrell & Sons of Thetford in 1928.

The most glamorous of them all, the Showman's Road Locomotive, pristine paintwork and adorned with the trademark polished twisted brass canopy supports. Used by travelling showmen to haul their caravans and fairground rides in multi trailer road trains around the country. Once set up, the fairground attraction would be powered by electricity generated by the belt-driven dynamo mounted on the smokebox extension. As road surfaces improved, solid rubber tyres became a standard fitment.

The steam ploughing engine revolutionised farming as large areas of arable farmland could now be cultivated in a relatively short period of time compared with that taken by horse drawn implements. Various methods were tried but the most common and efficient was that which used a pair of ploughing engines, one at each side of the field, drawing the plough or cultivator by means of a wire rope attached to a winding drum mounted beneath the boiler of each engine. Fowler's of Leeds were not only the largest manufacturer of ploughing engines, but also developed the bi-directional balance plough. This early single cylinder example from Fowler's Steam Plough Works built in 1874, Works No. 2479, demonstrates the use of the winching drum whilst ploughing.

An unusual traction engine by virtue of the fact that is was built in Ipswich by Ransomes, Sims & Jeffries, Works No. 31066, in 1920 as a crane engine and spent most of its working life moving equipment around their works. It is seen here with a sawbench suspended from the crane jib.

The design of the Sentinel Waggon (Sentinel always used this spelling) was significantly different to that of other wagon manufacturers, having a much more 'modern' look, which can be attributed to the vertical boiler mounted in the cab and to the underetype engine slung beneath the chassis. Here, Sentinel S4 Waggon No.9192 built in 1935 passes through the village of Eastnor in Herefordshire.

Not strictly speaking 'traction engines' but nevertheless worthy of inclusion as being steam powered, steam being generated by a paraffin fired boiler beneath the bonnet, powering an orthodox twin cylinder reciprocating slide valve engine mounted beneath the chassis. Seen here are two examples of steam cars from American manufacturer Stanley, who in 25 years of manufacturing produced nearly 11,000 vehicles, ceasing production in 1924 with the advance of the internal combustion engine.

THE RALLY SCENE

A scene that has become commonplace at most traction engine rallies, the traditional line up of participating engines in the grand parade ring, an opportunity for photographers and visitors to admire the many subtle shapes and sizes of engines from different manufacturers.

Marshall Traction Engine 37690 'Old Timer', the engine that began the traction engine rally movement as we know it today. Little did Arthur Napper know that when he took part and won that race for 'A Firkin of Ale' at Appleford in 1950, that what followed would be the start of a whole new phenomenon that is the traction engine rally enjoyed by countless thousands every year. 'Old Timer' is seen here at the 50th anniversary celebration of that race at Appleford in July 2000 when the Marshall was within two years of reaching 100 years of age.

1919-built Wallis & Steevens Expansion Engine 7683 *'Eileen the Erring'* competed in the second race for 'A Firkin of Ale' held at Nettlebed in June 1951, only to be beaten by the victorious *'Old Timer'*. The Wallis & Steevens did however share the limelight at the 50th anniversary celebration.

For the most part traction engine rallies are held on farm- or park-land during the summer months, when, even with our unpredictable weather, the land is dry enough for movement of exhibits and visitors alike. The Banbury Steam Society has for many years held its rally on farmland at Bloxham near Banbury. Blessed with fine weather, sole surviving Savage General Purpose Engine No. 474 *'Eliza'* built in Kings Lynn in 1889 pauses in a quite corner of the rally-field.

'Hildary' a 1920-built Ruston & Hornsby General Purpose Engine No. 115100 stands in a picturesque corner of the Hartington Moor Showground on the weekend of the Queen's Golden Jubilee Bank Holiday in 2002.

Opposite: After an extensive rebuild, only completed on the eve of the rally, 1908-built Robey 5NHP General Purpose Engine No. 28094, makes a welcome return to the Bloxham Rally, thirty years to the day since it first appeared with the present owner.

Clubs and societies are at times required to move the venue of their rally due to a variety of reasons. One such society, the Ross-on-Wye Steam Engine Society held a number of rallies at Upton on Severn, before moving to and purchasing their present site at Welland. Seen here at the Upton site is unusual vertical boiler tandem Marshall roller, Works No. 87125 built in 1933.

The Rushmoor Rally, an event to have fallen by the wayside was held at the former Army Showground at Rushmoor near Aldershot. Beautifully turned-out Garrett 4CD Showman's Tractor 'Countess' Works No. 32969 built in 1917 stands next to a similarly pristine living van complete with hanging flower baskets.

An unusual visitor to the Bloxham Rally, Aveling & Porter Tractor *'Dougal'* No. 6021 built in 1906 with its overall canopy and steam locomotive pattern spectacle plate.

Whilst the mainland UK is the stronghold of the traction engine rally, Southern Ireland has a large number of traction engine enthusiasts and engine owners. One of the premier events to be held is the Stradbally Rally in Co. Laois. Irish-registered Clayton & Shuttleworth Works No. 43173 built in 1910 is seen here at a Stradbally.

Shuttleworth House in Bedfordshire forms one of the most imposing backdrops of any rally site. Seen here is Garrett Wagon 34841 built in 1929 whilst attending the Old Warden Rally.

Aveling & Porter Tractor 5917 of 1906 in a typical rural setting at a small rally at Hanbury in Worcestershire.

The Pickering Rally in North Yorkshire was for many years the largest event in Northern England attracting a wide variety of exhibits. One such exhibit is unusual 1907-built Fowler Tractor No. 10773, which was originally exported to Australia.

In stark contrast to the International Air Tattoo held at the nearby RAF Fairford airbase, the Fairford Traction Engine Rally is a more tranquil affair held in serene parkland. Here Marshall Traction Engine *'The Alderman'* 28922 of 1897 is in the company of a selection of classic vehicles.

Some events are organised to benefit local charities, in this instance at Wellesbourne Water Mill in Warwickshire where the local Lions Club were the beneficiaries. Here 8 ton Fowler roller No.21629 built in1937 owned by the Hockley Heath Steam Association is seen being driven by a female member.

Seen here at the Appleford celebrations is Sentinel DG4 Waggon Works No. 8571 built in 1931 owned and painted in the livery of Morris Oils.

Opposite: An interesting scenario in that Clayton & Shuttleworth No. 46817 built in 1914 is seen here in front of Shuttleworth House, the former home of one of the company's founders.

Nestling beneath the trees on the Belvoir Castle estate is 1924-built Garrett Tractor No. 34461 'Victoria'.

Arriving at the Fairford Rally is Garrett 10 ton roller 'The Baroness' No. 34084 built in 1922 towing a living van and water cart.

The Old Warden Rally in Bedfordshire encompasses not only the Shuttleworth House parkland, but also adjacent farmland. Foden six wheel Tractor No. 13008 built in 1928 stands in a recently harvested cornfield.

Clayton and Shuttleworth No. 36731 of 1904 *'Old Glory'* against the imposing backdrop of Belvoir Castle.

It is the diversity of locations for traction engine rallies that is often the appeal for exhibitors and visitors alike. In recent years the Stroud Vintage Transport and Engine Club have held their annual Steam and Vintage Extravaganza on the former RAF airfield at Kemble in Gloucestershire. A pair of mothballed Tristar aircraft make an impressive backdrop for the1914-built Aveling & Porter GND Showman's Tractor *'Princess Victoria'* Works No. 19782.

1898 Burrell No. 2147 *'Old Lytham'* poses for the camera in front of Shuttleworth House at Old Warden.

What was formerly the Bishop's Castle Rally was, for a short period, held at Walcot Hall in Shropshire which provides the backdrop for Clayton & Shuttleworth 10 ton roller No. 46688 built in 1912.

Seen at an Old Warden Rally is this 1911-built Garrett 'Olive' No. 29764, the unusual design of smokebox indicates that this engine is superheated, a feature not usually found on traction engines.

Beautifully turned out Wallis & Steevens 5 ton Tractor 'Duke of Wellington' No. 7872 built in 1930 awaits its call for the grand parade at the Fairford Rally.

A typical 'Old Tyme' fairground recreation at the Bloxham Rally. 1914-built Burrell No. 3489 *'King George VI'* is prepared ready for powering the 'Big Wheel'.

A remarkable line-up of three different designs from the Mann Patent Steam Cart and Wagon Co. Ltd. From left to right, wagon No.1120 built in 1916, wagon No.1365 built in 1919, and tractor No.1386 built in 1919 at an Old Warden Rally.

Opposite: The chance to test steam power against the purpose-built diesel-powered tractors in the Tractor Pulling Arena at the Welland Rally was too good an opportunity to miss. Visiting from New Zealand, Burrell General Purpose single cylinder engine No. 3148 built in 1909 tests its strength against the purpose built sled.

The Much Marcle Rally site has the benefit of being able to provide an area for a steam ploughing demonstration, which is always a popular attraction. Fowler BB1 Ploughing Engine No. 15333 built in 1919 is seen here with a four furrow anti-balance plough.

One of only two surviving Burrell Ploughing Engines, *'The Earl'* Works No. 777 built in 1879 is still going strong demonstrating steam ploughing at a Bedfordshire rally.

One of only five surviving examples from manufacturers T.Green & Sons, 8 ton roller No. 1968 of 1917 drives gently around the parade ring, which is a feature of most traction engine rallies.

Garrett Showman's Tractor *'Margaret'* No. 33091 built in 1917 is entirely at home posed next to the 'Galloping Horses' fairground ride at a Vintage Gala held at the Gloucestershire Warwickshire Steam Railway at Toddington.

ON THE ROAD

A feature of a number of rallies is the Saturday evening 'Road Run' in which a number of exhibitors take the opportunity to take their engines away from the rally site for a short tour of the surrounding countryside and villages. Here a cavalcade of engines led by Super Sentinel Waggon No. 8381 head down the country lane away from the Tallington Rally near Stamford in Lincolnshire.

Whilst engines from far afield are invariably transported to rallies on low-loaders, part of the enjoyment for local exhibitors is to 'road' their engines to the event. Here Burrell 10 ton roller *'Ventongimps'* Works No. 4012 built in 1925 passes through the village of Bloxham in Oxfordshire.

1916-built 7NHP Ransomes, Sims & Jefferies Traction Engine *'Mendip Lady'* Works No. 26995 passes the Old Customs House at Ipswich Docks, heading for the now closed Tolly Cobbold Brewery.

Spring is in the air as Burrell *'Keeling'* No. 3121 built in 1909 passes through the Worcestershire countryside.

Burrell Showman's Road Locomotive *'Earl Kitchener'* No. 3651 built in 1915 passes Lew Church heading for Lechlade.

Wallis & Steevens Advance roller Works No. 8082 built in 1931 climbs into the Malvern Hills, returning home to Eastnor Castle.

In the livery of McMullen's Brewery 1932-built Sentinel DG4 No. 8694 passes the Holy Trinity church at Littlebury.

Opposite: 'The Badger' Burrell Road Locomotive No. 3941 built in 1923 passes through the village of Offchurch in Warwickshire.

Marshall General Purpose Engine No. 61970 built in 1913 pauses to refill with water at Bardwell in Suffolk.

'*Fair Rosamund*' Wallis & Steevens Expansion Engine No. 7370 of 1914 leaves the village of Tysoe in Warwickshire.

Burrell Showman's Road Locomotive *'Lady Pride of England'* No. 2625 built in 1904 at Castlemorton Common heading back from the Welland Rally.

Aveling & Barford 10 ton roller Works No. AC 604 built in 1937 climbs away from Welford on Avon in Warwickshire.

Foden Tractor No. 14078 built in 1932, after a heavy shower of rain.

Marshall General Purpose Engine *'Eynsham Hall'* No. 15391 built in 1887 passes through Bampton in Oxfordshire.

Whilst Babcock & Wilcox applied their own 'maker's plate', this 6 ton roller was built by Clayton & Shuttleworth in 1926, Works No. 95/4009 and is seen on an evening road run from the Tallington Rally.

The autumn colours of Hungerford Park complement the livery of Burrell Showman's Road Locomotive 'The Philadelphia' No. 3413 built in 1912.

Fowler R3 Traction Engine No. 18539 built in 1929 heads for Lechlade on a fine autumn day.

Taking part in the Great Eastern Road Run is Fowler A9 Road Locomotive No. 15467 *'Sir Douglas'* built in 1920.

Opposite: An unmistakable feature of the Cornish landscape is the remains of the lead and copper mining industry. Marshall 12 ton roller No. 88096 built in 1937 passes the remains of the South Wheal Towan copper mines at Porthtowan.

The crew of Fowler Agricultural No. 8282 'Berkeswell' built in 1899 look longingly at the country inn wishing that the hostelry was open on this hot summer morning.

Opposite: In a beautiful spring setting a convoy of engines led by Aveling & Porter 8 ton roller No. 10392 of 1922 pass through the village of Sambourne.

Doing the job for which it was designed, heavy haulage, Fowler B6 Road Locomotive *'Atlas'* No. 17105 built in 1928 crosses Castlemorton Common hauling a transformer trailer and living van in convoy with a couple of period buses.

A scene which would have been commonplace in the working days of a steam roller, heading through countryside to the next roadmaking contract.   Ruston & Hornsby 12 ton roller No. 114059 built in 1921 towing a Bomford & Evershed living van near Hook Norton in Oxfordshire.

Ruston Proctor General Purpose Engine Works No. 33189 of 1907 takes a leisurely early evening drive through the village of Greatford in Lincolnshire. The metal straked wheels on this engine are not ideal for today's hard surfaced roads.

Opposite: With the glorious backdrop of Porthtowan, 1916-built Super Sentinel Waggon No. 1465 storms 'Engine Hill'.

An end of season outing around Little Chalfont for Fowler 12 ton roller *'Arfur'* No. 18659 built in 1930.

Passing through Gamlingay in Bedfordshire, Burrell Showman's Road Locomotive 'Nero' No. 3669 of 1915 with a period Showman's Living Van.

Heading out into the Warwickshire lanes for the first outing of the season's *'Tomboy'*, a 1926-built Wallis & Steevens Advance 10 ton roller Works No. 7905.

Garrett 4CD Tractor No. 33981 of 1920 towing a Marshall threshing drum heads for home after attending a NTET driving experience weekend at the Hatton Craft Centre in Warwickshire.

The participants of the Society of Drivers and Enginemen end of season road run in Oxfordshire, pause for lunch at the Clanfield Tavern, leaving 1894-built Aveling & Porter R10 class 10 ton roller No. 3430 built in 1894 simmering by the roadside.

'Sister Wendy', 1931 Ransomes, Sims & Jeffries Traction Engine No. 42013 effortlessly surmounts 'Engine Hill' at Porthtowan in Cornwall. The former Cornish mining engine house in the background is now a private residence.

OUT AND ABOUT

A scene dating back to 1988, when Fowler single cylinder Ploughing Engines No. 2861 of 1876 and No. 3195 of 1877 together with Robey Traction Engine *'King George V'* No. 29450 of 1910 await their fate in a farmyard in Worcestershire. To date the Robey still awaits restoration whilst the pair of ploughing engines are now fully restored and can be regularly seen demonstrating steam ploughing.

Garrett Tractor *'Evelyn'* built in 1924 Works No. 34539 is seen here at the East Anglian Railway Museum at Chappel and Wakes Colne Station in Essex.

72

1902-built Fowell Works No. 91 is the oldest surviving example from this low volume Huntingdonshire manufacturer. Seen here against the picturesque backdrop of Old Warden village hall.

Seen in the grounds of the former rectory at Cadeby, home of steam enthusiast the late Reverend 'Teddy' Boston, is Foster Traction Engine *'Fiery Alice'* No. 14593 of 1927, being prepared for an open day at the rectory.

Opposite: This angler seems to be totally oblivious to the passing of Burrell Road Locomotive *'Clinker'* Works No. 3257 of 1911 over the Grantham Canal at Woolsthorpe.

The driver of Marshall Traction Engine *'Margaret'* No. 51025 of 1908 will need to observe caution when moving away from the thatched cottage in this scene in the village of Honnington in Warwickshire.

Seen at the Wellesbourne Water Mill, this replica Hovis bread van is powered by a twin cylinder Locomobile steam car engine, steam being produced by a vertical paraffin-fuelled boiler.

The magnificent Cotswold Stone Stanway House in Gloucestershire is the backdrop for 1889 Hornsby Traction Engine 'Maggie' Works No. 6557.

Fowler TE2 Haulage and Winching Engine No. 14950 built in 1918 was part of a cancelled order for the Russian Government and was subsequently sold to the War Department. The engine carries a small under-the-boiler horizontal winch not usually fitted to a road engine. Seen here in the delightful setting of the village of Eastnor with the Parish Church of St John the Baptist as a backdrop.

A chance encounter whilst on a visit to the Isle of Man found Marshall 10 ton Compound Roller No. 75408 built in 1922 for the Isle of Man Highways Board. Now privately owned the roller is seen here compacting the driveway to the old water mill in Castletown.

This Foden C-type Tanker No. 13316 of 1929, was built originally as a tar sprayer before conversion to a ballast box body and has now reverted back to a tanker. Seen here at the Burley Cider Making Weekend at Burley in the New Forest.

Aveling & Porter 'C' Type 10 ton roller No. 11956 built in 1927 is seen here against a backdrop of the farm near Goathland in North Yorkshire, used as a location in the popular TV series 'Heartbeat'.

A blaze of autumn colours welcomes Burrell Showman's Road Locomotive 'Nancy' Works No. 3288 built in 1911 in the gardens of Stanway House in the Cotswolds.

Built by Arthur Trotter in 1933 this unusual vertical-boilered one ton roller was used by the builder for rolling the paths around his estate. Now in the custody of the City of Gloucester Folk Museum, the roller has a rare outing at Eastnor Castle.

This Sentinel S4 Waggon built in 1934 Works No. 9074 is named *'Proctor's Pride'* after its original restorer Ted Proctor, a former Sentinel driver. Seen here preparing for departure from Little Chalfont on an autumn road run.

Under a threatening sky 1928-built Tasker Tractor No.1928 built in 1928 prepares to leave the village of Chenies in Hertfordshire.

A Spring Transport Gala at Buckfastleigh on the South Devon Railway found Aveling & Porter 10 ton 'F' type roller No.10824 built in 1923 in the station forecourt.

Burrell 'Devonshire' Traction Engine *'Jellicoe'* Works No. 3368 built in 1912 displayed in the sunshine on the occasion of a visit by the Road Locomotive Society to the collection of Richard Willcox in Gloucestershire. Note that the rear wheels have been fitted with rubber strakes.

Youngest surviving example of a Foden Tractor *'Duchess of Gloucester'* built in 1933 Works No. 14084 heads away from a local charity event near Leamington Spa.

Pictures of the water mill in the Cotswold village of Lower Slaughter have appeared in numerous publications, but few, if any, have featured a traction engine in this idyllic setting. Built as a roller in 1931 Fowler Works No.19456 *'Highland Lass'* has been converted into a tractor and is proudly displayed by the River Eye.

Burrell Showman's Road Locomotive *'Princess Mary'* built in 1922 Works No. 3949 proudly stands next to Carters Steam Yachts during the visit of Carters Steam Fair to Pinkneys Green in Berkshire.

The N.T.E.T. driving experience weekend gives non-engine-owning members the opportunity to drive traction engines under supervision in a safely controlled environment. Here the owner of 1898-built Burrell Traction Engine *'Old Lytham'* No. 2112 explains the finer points of engine control to a participant at a driver experience weekend in Worcestershire.

1917-built Foden Tipping Wagon No. 7758 attends a 'steam party' at Eastnor Castle in Herefordshire.

'E' class Aveling & Porter 10 ton roller built in 1923 as Works No.10556 is seen against the backdrop of Belvoir Castle.

The village of Eastnor in Herefordshire has numerous photographic opportunities. Garrett 4CD Tractor No. 33981 of 1920 pauses by the village green.

'Winifrid' a Burrell Road Locomotive built in 1919 Works No. 3809 is seen here near Stonehouse in Gloucestershire.

Ransomes, Sims & Jeffries Traction Engine No. 26839 built in 1915 in 'working' condition together with a former Herefordshire County Council living van seen here in parkland near Ledbury.

Seen here in a typical farmyard setting near Hatton in Warwickshire is *'Princess Mary'* a 1918-built Garrett Tractor No. 33278.

Opposite: The crew of third oldest surviving Aveling & Porter, 1884-built Traction Engine No. 1995 and LMS Railway dray take the opportunity for an evening tour of the Belvoir Castle estate.

Whilst the parishioners take Holy Communion at the Parish Church of St John the Baptist in Eastnor, Garrett Showman's Tractor' *Margaret'* No. 33091 built in 1917 pauses whilst en route to Eastnor Castle.

For a number of years the author maintained and rallied this ex Coventry Corporation 6 ton patching roller built by Aveling Barford in 1938 Works No. AC 624. Seen here in the Warwickshire village of Armscote.

Marshall General Purpose Engine No. 61970 built in 1913 is captured here in this industrial scene at the Buckinghamshire Railway Centre at Quainton Road Station.

The ex Anderton & Rowlands Fowler B6 'Super Lion' Showman's Road Locomotive *'The Lion'* Works No. 19782 built in 1932, seen in the grounds of Stanway House.

The gatehouse at Eastnor Castle provides a magnificent backdrop for 1920-built Foden Wagon No. 10320.

Marshall 'Q' type No. 76301 built originally in 1923 as a roller is seen here carrying out a lake dredging operation in Crogga Woods in the Isle of Man.

Built by John Allen Ltd of Oxford in 1898 from Fowler parts this unique roller is ensuring that the going is 'good to firm' at Stratford Racecourse.

'Dorothy' Works No. 4093 built in 1931 was the last road locomotive built by Charles Burrell & Sons and is seen at the preserved Quainton Road Station in Buckinghamshire.

Of all the ploughing engines built by Fowlers the Z7 is the largest of them all weighing in at over 26 tons. Built in 1922 this engine was one of a number of Z7's exported to the Sena Sugar Estates in Mozambique. Returned to the UK and restored to full working condition, No. 15670 is working here along with a four furrow plough.

Spring is in the air as oldest surviving Garrett 'Lucy' No. 23992 built in 1902 arrives at the Avoncroft Museum in Worcestershire.

The sun rises over Hollowell in Northampton-shire on the morning of the NTET 50th Anniversary Road Run. The fire has yet to be lit in Allchin Traction Engine No. 1546 *'Rebel'* built in 1912.

ENGINES AT WORK

The steam roller can, on occasions, still be called upon to carry out useful work for which it was designed. Not so much for road construction with hot asphalt, but for compacting stone in car parks and driveways. Here Fowler 10 ton roller No. 20122 built in 1933 is seen rolling a freshly laid stone car park.

Before the advent of the combine harvester, the corn crop would firstly be cut and trussed into sheaves for storage in ricks and then secondly, the grain would be separated from the straw by a threshing machine usually owned by a contractor. A traction engine would be used to not only power the threshing machine, but also to haul it from farm to farm. Here Marshall Traction Engine 'Punch' Works No. 36258 built in 1902 is used to power the Clayton threshing machine at Old Warden.

Opposite: An unusual Robinson horizontal frame saw is seen here being driven by a 12NHP Marshall Portable Engine No. 69778 built in 1916.

Horsedrawn Merryweather steam firepump *'Blenheim'* dating from 1890 is seen here pumping water from the River Dene at Wellesbourne in Warwickshire. This firepump was originally employed on the Blenheim Palace estate in Oxfordshire and for a number of years was in the custody of the retained firemen at Shipston on Stour.

Opposite: In rural Herefordshire a pair of Fowler Ploughing Engines are employed in dredging out accumulated silt from a lake. Here the scoop is being drawn across the bed of the lake by the engine on the opposite bank, whilst the wire rope is drawn from the winching drum of Fowler BB1 No. 15333 of 1919, which in turn will draw the scoop back across the lake, scouring the lake bed as it goes.

On a beautiful summer afternoon in rural Warwickshire, Fowler AA7 Ploughing Engine No15257 built in 1918 simmers as the four furrow balance plough sets off across the field winched by the second ploughing engine.

1901-built Aveling & Porter 10 ton roller No. 4872 in the beautiful Cotswold surroundings of Stanway House rolling in a freshly laid Cotswold stone courtyard. Payment for this contract was by way of a firkin of ale brewed at the Stanway Brewery situated at Stanway House.

In a vain attempt to compete with the advance of the internal-combustion-engined tractor, Garretts produced this tractor in 1919, Works No. 33180 *'The Suffolk Punch'* for use in direct ploughing as demonstrated here.

Opposite: In the depths of winter Fowler AA7 Ploughing Engine *'Sandringam'* No. 15365 built in 1919 is commercially employed dredging a lake in Ledbury.

The unique J & F Howard Ploughing Engine *'The Farmer's Engine'* built in the 1870s is unusual in having the winching drum mounted horizontally across the rear of the engine. The engine is seen here taking part in the Great Ploughing Challenge at Boddington.

A Showman's Road Locomotive generating electricity after dark is an experience to behold. Burrell *'Majestic'* No.3890 built in 1922 demonstrates the ability to produce electricity from the belt-driven dynamo to full effect.

Doing the job for which it was designed, heavy haulage, Fowler B6 Road Locomotive 'Atlas' No. 17105 built in 1928 hauling a transformer trailer. On this occasion 'Atlas' was being driven by legendary steeplejack, the late Fred Dibnah.

GREAT DORSET STEAM FAIR

The heavy haulage demonstration is a spectacle that has become such a part of the Great Dorset Steam Fair and one that will not be seen anywhere else. Four road locomotives, three of which are crane engines are coupled together hauling a low-loader carrying a steam locomotive around the arena.

Nowhere else in the world can a visitor find so many Showman's Engines in one place at any one time as can be found at the Great Dorset Steam Fair. Ex Anderton & Rowlands Burrell Showman's Road Locomotive No. 3912 'Dragon' built in 1921 is but one of up to seventy Showman's Engines on site.

Demonstrations involving the use of traction engines as they would have been used in their working life are a popular attraction. Here the threshing demonstration is in full swing – McLaren *'The Favourite'* No. 1105 built in 1910 is driving the rare Foden threshing machine.

'Old Nick' a 1908-built Marshall No. 49725 attended the Great Dorset Steam Fair as part of the Marshall themed year.

With the shadows lengthening, Fowler BB1 Ploughing Engine 'Lady Jayne' No. 15334 built in 1919 together with a cultivator have finished work for the day.

Burrell Showman's Road Locomotive 'Quo Vadis' No. 3938 built in 1922 has long been the 'flagship engine' of the Great Dorset Steam Fair and is proudly listed as entry No.1 in the show programme each year.

The year 2000 event was billed as the Burrell Millennium Special attracting a huge number of Burrell exhibits which included five visiting engines from New Zealand, one of which was this 8NHP Burrell General Purpose Engine No.3529 built in 1913 which spent all of its working life threshing.

Many of the Old Tyme Fair rides are powered by the electricity generated by the Showman's Engines. Fowler B6 Showman's Road Locomotive *'Supreme'* No. 20223 of 1934, the last Showman's Road Locomotive to be built by Fowlers, stands ready for work.

Opposite: A practical demonstration of road making is carried out which is further enhanced by the associated paraphernalia.

Unusual Super Sentinel Tractor No. 5644 *'The Elephant'* built in 1924 was a visitor from the Netherlands. One other example of this tractor survives in South Africa.

Probably the most famous Showman's Road Locomotive *'The Iron Maiden'*. Built originally in 1920 as a Road Locomotive No. 15657 *'Kitchener'*, the engine was later converted by Fowlers to a Showman's Road Locomotive, and was renamed *'The Iron Maiden'* in 1962 after taking the starring role in film of the same name. Seen here taking a tour around the Dorset arena before rejoining the evening line up of Showman's Engines.

A popular attraction at the Old Tyme Fair are Harry Lees Steam Yachts, *'Columbia'* and *'Shamrock'*, built by Savage Bros in 1901. The yachts are powered by a swing engine also built by Savage Bros.

Coupled to a Burrell Traction Engine and hauling a heavy timber trailer, Ransomes, Sims & Jefferies Traction Engine *'Winifred'* built in 1903 No. 15127 blasts up the hill from 'Watford Gap' in the Heavy Haulage Arena.

As night falls the atmosphere of the Great Dorset Steam Fair becomes electric as the Showman's Road Locomotives come into their own. Under a full moon Burrell *'Lord Lascelles'* Works No. 3886 built in 1921 gently generates power under an array of canopy bulbs.

The site of the GDSF is not a permanent showground, but takes place each year on 700 acres of arable farmland after harvesting at Tarrant Hinton in Dorset. Here Fowler BB1 Ploughing Engine No. 15139 'Master' built in 1918 is set against the rolling Dorset countryside.

Built by in 1914 as a wagon, this Foden No. 4258 was rebuilt from a derelict state into a steam omnibus and is regular visitor to the Great Dorset Steam Fair giving visitors the opportunity to ride around the arena.

Burrell Traction Engine 'Pride of Devon' No. 4014 built in 1925 is shown here in a wonderful work-stained patina, driving the rack sawbench in the woodsawing demonstration area.

'Boadicea', McLaren Road Locomotive No. 1652 built in 1919, demonstrates the power of the road locomotive by moving unassisted the low-loader transporter loaded with the steam locomotive, a total weight approaching 140 tons.

A Showman's Road Locomotive generating after dark is an experience to behold particularly when in the company of up to fifty other engines doing likewise. Burrell 'Island Chief' No. 3878 built in 1921, gently rocks back and forth with the motion of the crankshaft, whilst the dynamo gently hums away.

The Great Dorset Steam Fair has a unique atmosphere, found nowhere else in the steam preservation world.

The sun sets at the end of yet another day at the Great Dorset Steam Fair.

BITS AND PIECES

The final polish is given to the copper chimney cap of the Aveling & Porter Road Locomotive before the day's events.

The cylinder block and valve gear on 1919-built Wallis & Steevens 'expansion' engine.

Opposite: Polished brass and gleaming paintwork are synonymous with the Showman's Road Locomotive.

A traditional brass traction engine paraffin headlamp.

'It's a dog's life'.

A study of concentration from the driver of the McLaren Ploughing Engine.

A study of steam and sunlight.

Left: The Foster wagon catches the golden light from the setting sun.

A builder's plate from Bomford & Evershed who were not only Worcestershire-based steam rolling contractors but were also builders of living vans.

Right: A brass lamp receives a final polish from an attentive owner.

Two examples of our glorious heritage, a Marshall Traction Engine overlooked by Belvoir Castle.